Electric Bass

By Roger Filiberto

1

57

10.95 EACH

THIS BOOK IS THE ANSWER TO MANY REQUESTS FOR A THOROUGH AND CAREFULLY GRADED APPROACH TO THE ELECTRIC BASS.

THIS INSTRUMENT HAS ATTAINED GREAT HEIGHTS WITH ONLY A LIMITED AMOUNT OF INSTRUCTIONAL MATERIAL AVAILABLE.

WE HIGHLY RECOMMEND THIS BOOK TO ANYONE DESIROUS OF PLAYING THE ELECTRIC BASS AS A MUSICIAN.

Mel Bay

CD Contents

1. Tune Up {1:09}
2. Diatonic Passage in "C" {:24}
3. More Diatonic Passage in "C" {:18}
4. Lightly Row {:52}
5. Careless Love {:49}
6. Western Folk Song {:54}
7. Cielito Lindo {:37}
8. "Boogie" in C {:35}
9. On Top of Old Smokey {1:09}
10. Walking the Bass {:43}
11. Saints Come Marching In {:40}
12. Twelve Bar Boogie in "C" {:34}
13. More Boogie in "C" {:41}
14. Eight to the Bar Boogie in "G" {:27}
15. More Eight Bar Boogie {:26}
16. Eight Bar Blues in "G" {:27}
17. Italian Boat Song {:40}
18. Two "Circle of Sixths" Patterns {:50}
19. Example Using "F♯" {:48}
20. More in "C" {:29}
21. Still More in "C" {:29}
22. Rock n' Roll-Rhythm & Blues Boogie Patterns {2:03}
23. Four Bar Blues Pattern in "C" {:32}
24. Intro to Volume 2 {:14}
25. 16 Bar Walking Bass {:44}
26. Drink to Me Only with Thine Eyes {:57}
27. 12 Bar Blues Key of "D" {:50}
28. Keep Movin' #1 {1:17}
29. Walking Bass 3 Chord Pattern {:40}
30. Triplet Study in "D" {:36}
31. V Position Study {:32}
32. Boogie Beat in "C" {:59}
33. 3 Chord Blues Pattern in "G" {1:05}
34. 12 Bar Rhythm & Blues {:34}
35. Spooky Stuff {:44}
36. Relaxing {1:13}
37. Easy Does It {1:09}
38. Key Largo Blues {:47}
39. Typical Bass in F {1:09}
40. More Walking Bass 3 Chord Pattern {1:08}
41. Rhythm & Blues Pattern in "C" {1:04}
42. Walking Bass 3 Chord Pattern {1:06}
43. Tenths Study {:45}
44. Little Brown Jug {:42}
45. American Patrol {1:22}
46. For Further Study {:18}

Recording by Dino Monoxelos

This book is available either by itself or packaged with a companion audio and/or video recording. If you have purchased the book only, you may wish to purchase the recordings separately. The publisher strongly recommends using a recording along with the text to assure accuracy of interpretation and make learning easier and more enjoyable.

1 2 3 4 5 6 7 8 9 0

Visit us on the Web at www.melbay.com — E-mail us at email@melbay.com

ROGER FILIBERTO

Roger Fileberto needs no introduction to the guitar world as his students are some of the finest artists in America today.

For decades, he was a successful professional and teacher in New Orleans where he operated one of the top studious in this country.

Among his many contributions to the study of the guitar and bass guitar, this book is one of his finest.

TUNING THE ELECTRIC BASS

The four open strings of the Bass will be the same pitch as the four notes shown in the illustration of the piano keyboard. Note that all of the strings are below middle C of the piano keyboard.

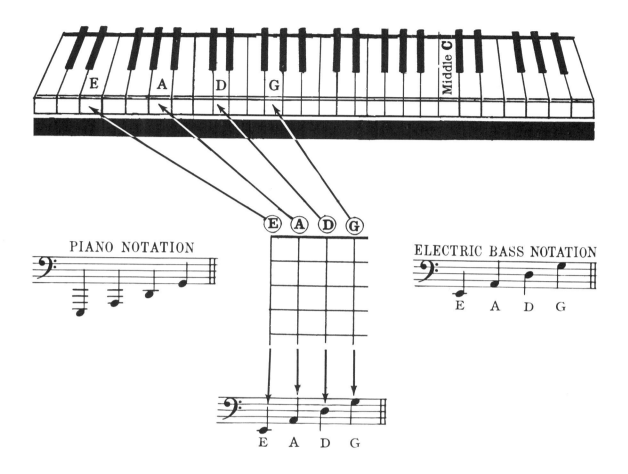

ANOTHER METHOD OF TUNING

1. Tune the 4th string in unison to the E or 19th white key to the left of middle C on the piano.

2. Place the finger behind the fifth fret of the 4th string. This will give you the tone or pitch of the 3rd string (A).

3. Place finger behind the fifth fret of the 3rd string to obtain the pitch of the 2nd string (D).

4. Place the finger behind the fifth fret of the 2nd string to obtain the pitch of the first string (G).

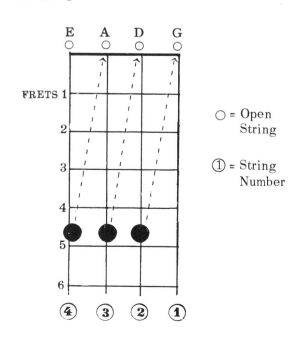

THE RUDIMENTS OF MUSIC

The Staff

Music is written on a STAFF consisting of FIVE LINES and FOUR SPACES.

The lines and spaces are numbered upward as shown:

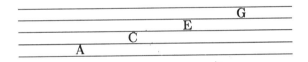

They also have LETTER names.

The LINES are names as follows: 1–G, 2–B, 3–D, 4–F, 5–A.

The letter-names of the SPACES are: 1–A, 2–C, 3–E, 4–G.

The Bass Clef

This sign ![bass clef] is the Bass Clef.

All Electric Bass Music will be written in this clef.

The STAFF is divided into MEASURES by vertical lines called BARS.

Double bars mark the end of a section or strain of music.

Notes

This is a NOTE:

A note has three parts.

They are -- the HEAD ●, the STEM |, and the FLAG ⌐.

Notes may be placed in the staff,

above the staff,

and

below the staff.

A note will bear the name of the line or space it occupies on the staff.

The location of a note in, above or below the staff will indicate the Pitch.

PITCH: the highness or lowness of a tone.

TONE: a musical sound.

This is a WHOLE NOTE **o** The head is hollow. It does not have a stem.	This is a HALF NOTE ♩ The head is hollow. It has a stem.
This is a QUARTER NOTE ♩ The head is solid. It has a stem.	This is an EIGHTH NOTE ♪ The head is solid. It has a stem and a flag.

Note Values

o = 4 BEATS A WHOLE-NOTE will receive Four Beats or Counts.	♩ = 2 BEATS A HALF-NOTE will receive Two Beats or Counts.	♩ = 1 BEAT A QUARTER NOTE will receive One Beat or Count.	♪ = ½ BEAT An EIGHTH-NOTE will receive One-half Beat or Count. (2 for 1 beat)

Rests

A REST is a sign used to designate a period of silence.

This period of silence will be of the same duration of time as the note to which it corresponds.

This is a WHOLE REST Note that it hangs DOWN from the line.	This is a HALF REST Note that it lays ON the line.
This is a QUARTER REST	This is an EIGHTH REST

Notes and Comparative Rests

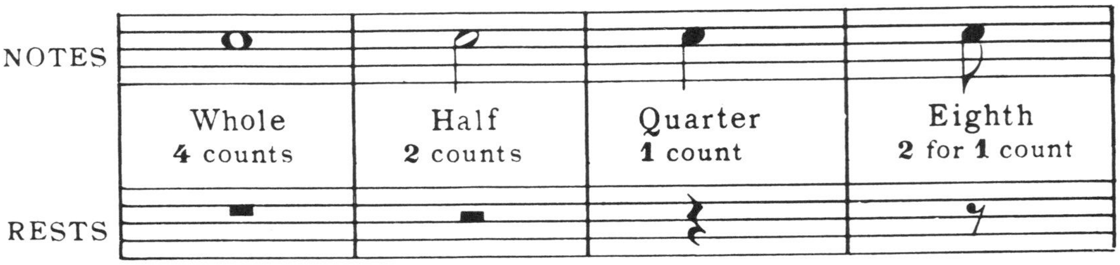
NOTES
Whole
4 counts
Half
2 counts
Quarter
1 count
Eighth
2 for 1 count
RESTS

The Time Signature

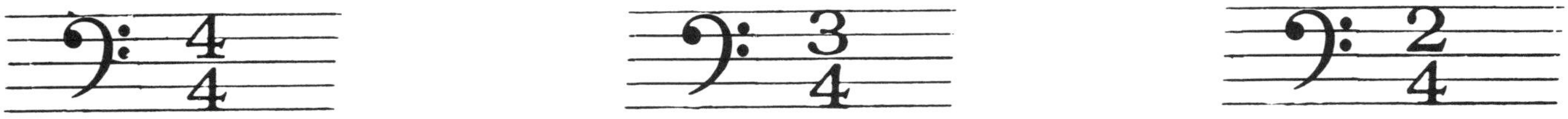

The above examples are the common types of time signatures to be used in this book.

4 – – The TOP NUMBER indicates the *number of beats per measure.*

4 – – The BOTTOM NUMBER indicates the *type of note receiving one beat.*

$\frac{4}{4}$ time and COMMON-TIME are the same.

4 – – beats per measure.

4 – – a quarter-note receives one beat.

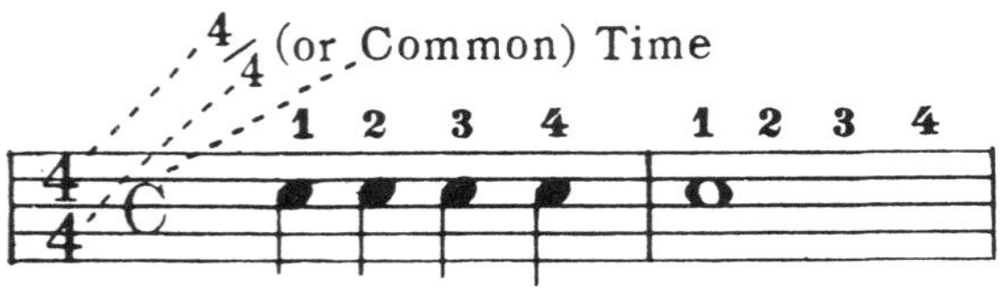
4/4 (or Common) Time
1 2 3 4 1 2 3 4

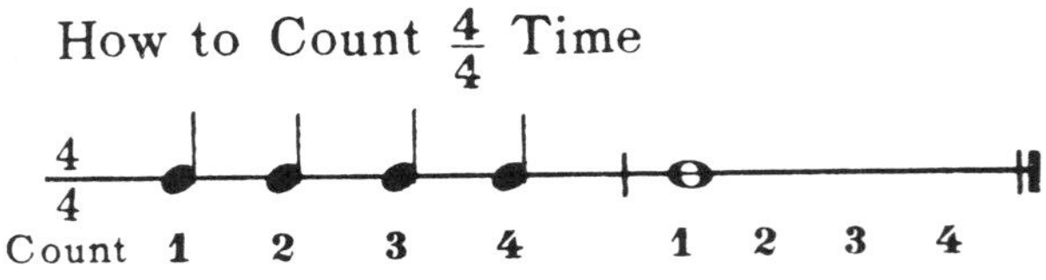
How to Count 4/4 Time
Count 1 2 3 4 1 2 3 4

Ledger Lines

When the pitch of a musical sound is below or above the staff, the notes are then placed on, or between, extra lines called LEDGER LINES.

They will be like this:

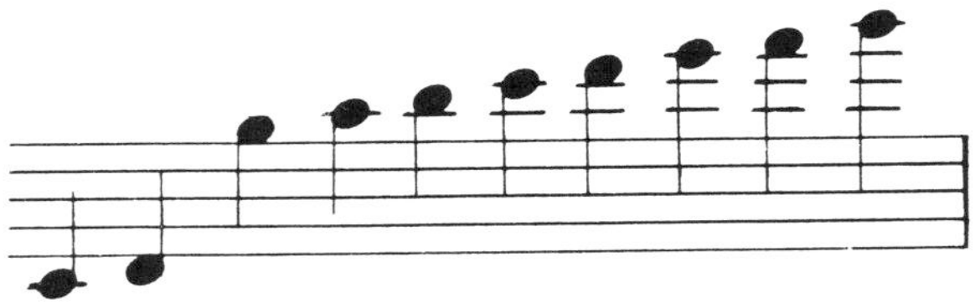

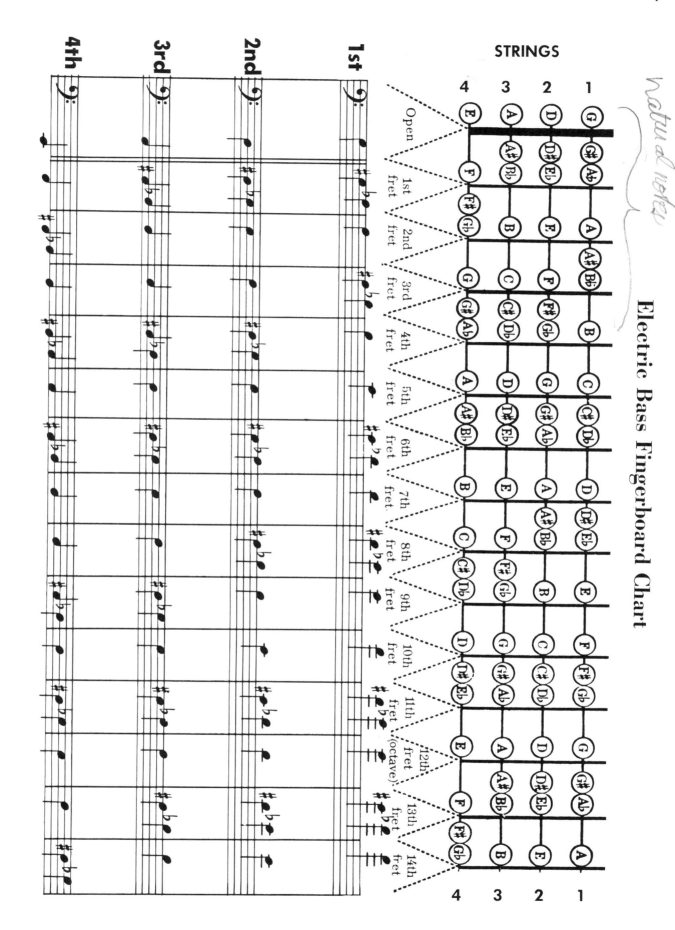

Electric Bass Fingerboard Chart

8

THE FINGERBOARD

The vertical lines are the strings.

The horizontal lines are the frets.

The encircled numbers

④ ③ ② ①

are the number of the strings.

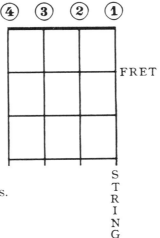

④ ③ ② ①

FRET

STRING

This Is the Pick

The Left Hand

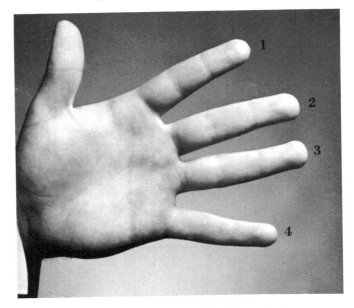

1
2
3
4

The Left Hand Position

Holding the Bass

The Right Hand

The strings of the Electric Bass are generally sounded by the first and second fingers of the right hand. Some Bassist play with the thumb. We *do not* recommend the use of the thumb. Obviously one can develop more speed and execution with the first and second fingers.

The Position of the Right Hand

In the above illustrations you will note that the first and second fingers are held relatively straight, (slightly curved) at an almost 45 degree angle in the direction of the bridge. The thumb is held under the palm of the hand, near the 4th string and pointing downward in the direction of the bridge, in the same manner of the Jazz Bassist playing the Bass Viol with the fingers.

When striking the strings come to rest against the next lowest string. This method is called the Hammerstroke. (rest stroke)

Always bear in mind to alternate the fingers whenever possible and practical.

Study on Open Strings

In marking the right hand fingering we have endeavored to teach the student the use of the 1st and 2nd fingers of the Right Hand. In recommending "alternating the Right Hand fingers" it is not the author's intention to have the student feel that alternating should be followed to the letter. This choice of Right Hand fingering is flexible and the student should work out any fingering that is to his advantage. Try a passage starting with the 1st Right Hand finger and then try starting it with the 2nd finger. See which pattern feels more comfortable or workable. Use of correct fingers will become automatic in time.

. = 1st Finger of Right Hand
: = 2nd Finger of Right Hand

Whole Note Study

A whole note (o) receives four counts. It is struck on the first count and held for the remaining three. Use down stroke (⊓) only.

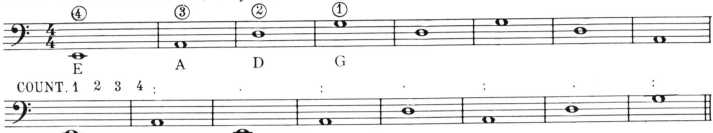

Half Note Study

The half note (♩) receives two counts. It is struck on the first count and held for the other.

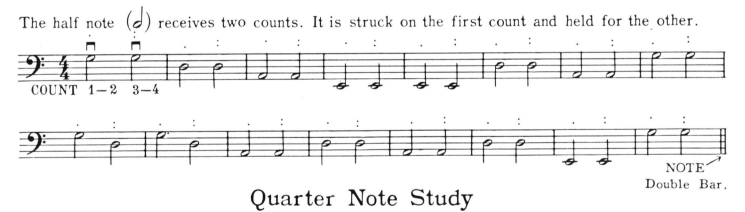

NOTE
Double Bar.

Quarter Note Study

A quarter note (♩) receives one count.

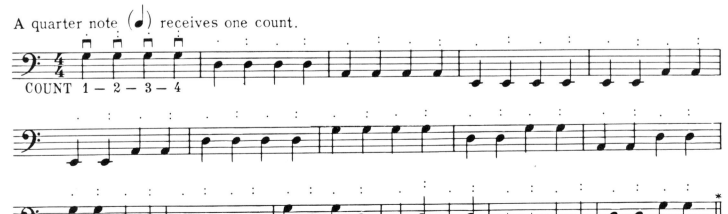

NOTE * A double bar (𝄇) at the end of an exercise or study denotes the end of the study.

NOTES ON THE FOURTH STRING ④

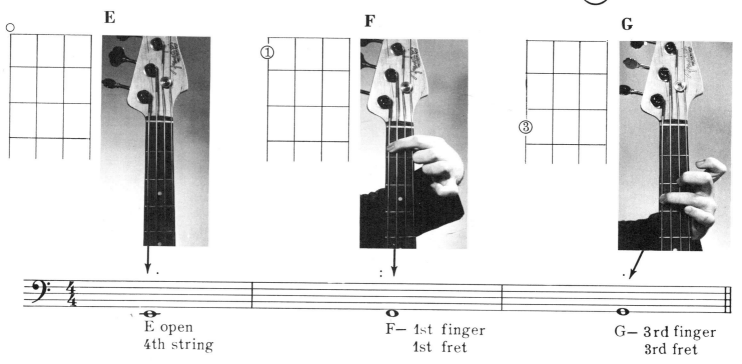

E open
4th string

F— 1st finger
1st fret

G— 3rd finger
3rd fret

Jump Off

COUNT 1—2—3—4

Half Time

COUNT 1—2 3—4

Speeding It Up

Introducing the repeat sign :‖

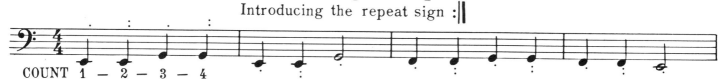

COUNT 1 — 2 — 3 — 4

Right Hand fingering same as above.

The two dots at the end
means to repeat the song or
exercise from the beginning.

For further study see
Electric Bass Position Studies
by Roger Filiberto

Continue to alternate 1st and 2nd fingers of Right Hand.

Dotted Half-Note

A dot (•) placed behind a note increases its value by one-half.

A dotted half-note (♩.) will receive three beats.

Three-Four Time

This sign  indicates three-four time.

3 -- beats per measure.
4 -- type of note receiving one beat (quarter note).

In three-four time, we will have three beats per measure.
A quarter note will receive one beat.

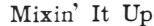

COUNT 1 2 3

Mixin' It Up

COUNT 1 2 3 4

Introducing the QUARTER REST 𝄽

A quarter rest (𝄽) has the same value as a quarter note (♩) and indicates one count of silence.

The New Comer

COUNT 1 2 3 4

R. H. fingering Simile

NOTE * Do not let the note before the rest ring past the one count value of the quarter note! Release finger pressure on quarter notes in order to get the full effect of the rest. If you have a teacher his explanation will make this lesson simple. . . . . If you do not have a teacher just use your judgement.

May 18
○ here

NOTES ON THE THIRD STRING ③

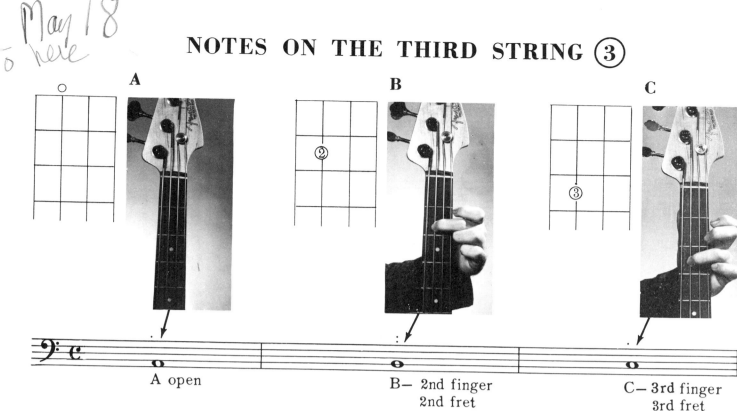

A open

B— 2nd finger
2nd fret

C— 3rd finger
3rd fret

A String Study
(WHOLE NOTE)

COUNT 1 – 2 – 3 – 4

Half Note Study

1 – 2   3 – 4

Quarter Note Study

1   2   3   4

Simile

Review on E and A String

1 2 3 4

Simile

14

More on A String

R. H. Simile

Repeat above study using this R. H. pattern : . : .

E and A String

R. H. Simile

Quiet Like

COUNT 1 2 3 4

Simile

Review

Simile

Repeat : . : .

Notes on E and A String

E	F	G	A	B	C
4th open	1st fret	3rd fret	3rd open	2nd fret	3rd fret

NOTES ON THE SECOND STRING ②

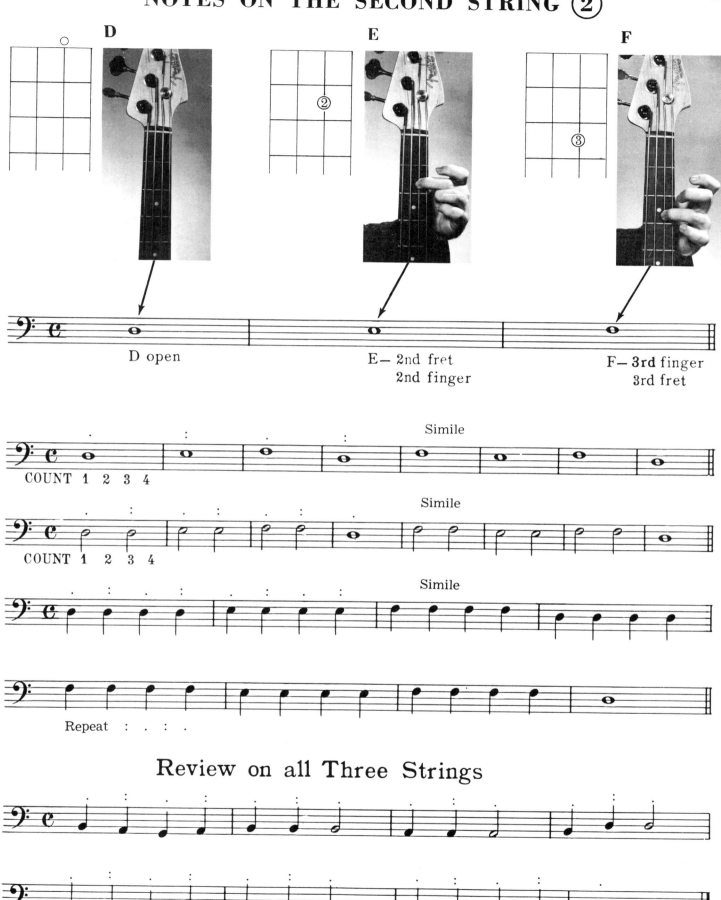

D

E

F

D open

E— 2nd fret
2nd finger

F— **3rd** finger
3rd fret

COUNT 1 2 3 4

Simile

COUNT 1 2 3 4

Simile

Simile

Repeat : . : .

Review on all Three Strings

NOTES ON THE FIRST STRING ①

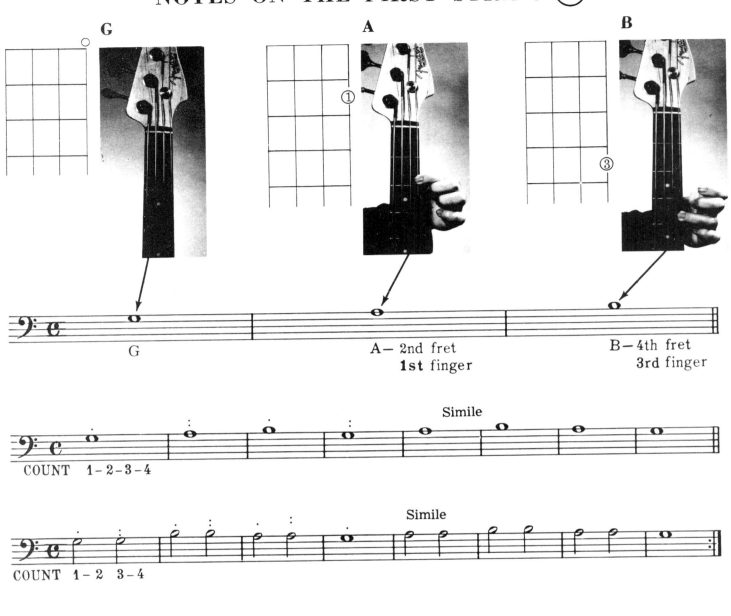

G   A   B

G

A— 2nd fret
1st finger

B— 4th fret
3rd finger

COUNT 1-2-3-4

COUNT 1-2 3-4

COUNT 1 — 2 — 3 — 4

Four String Review

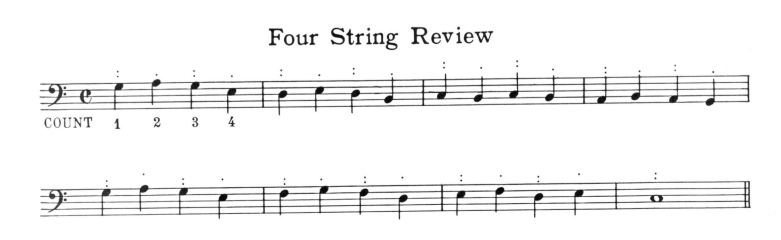

COUNT 1   2   3   4

THE "C" NOTE

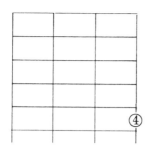

Play the "C" Note by placing the 4th finger behind the fifth fret of the first string.

	4th string			3rd string			2nd string			1st string			
	E	F	G	A	B	C	D	E	F	G	A	B	C
frets	open	1	3	open	2	3	open	2	3	0	2	4	5
fingering		1	3		2	3		2	3		1	3	4

(watch fingering)

THE KEY OF C

All music studied so far in this book has been in the Key of C.

That means that the notes have been taken from the C Scale (shown below) and made into melodies.

It is called the C Scale because the first note is C and we proceed through the musical alphabet until C reappears. C-D-E-F-G-A-B-C.

THE C SCALE

Ascending   Descending

Steps → 1   1   ½   1   1   1   ½

STEPS

A Half-Step is the distance from a given tone to the next higher or lower tone.

A Whole-Step consists of TWO Half-Steps.

The C Scale has two half-steps. They are between E-F and B-C.

Note the distance of one fret between those notes. The distances between C-D, D-E, F-G, G-A, and A-B are Whole-Steps.

DIATONIC PASSAGES IN C

MORE DIATONIC SEQUENCES

→ June 8

At this stage, student should try to work out R. H. fingering. Just remember to keep alternating fingers.

A Study in Thirds
KEY OF C

Lightly Row

The Tie

The TIE is a curved line between two notes of the same pitch.

The first note is played and held for the time duration of both.

The second note is not struck again but held.

Careless Love
Folk Song in C
INTRODUCING "WALKING BASS" PATTERN

Western Folk Song

Cielito Lindo

"Boogie" in C

The Repeat Sign

Dots before and after a double bar mean repeat the measures between.

On Top Of Old Smokey

Jun 15th

Walking the Bass
IN C

Saints Come Marching In

Study of Fifths in C

The study of fifths is most important. Fifths represent the alternating basses of the vast majority of chords as you will see later in the book, when you reach the section of the book relating to alternating bass study.

INTRODUCING THE SHARPS (♯) AND FLATS (♭)

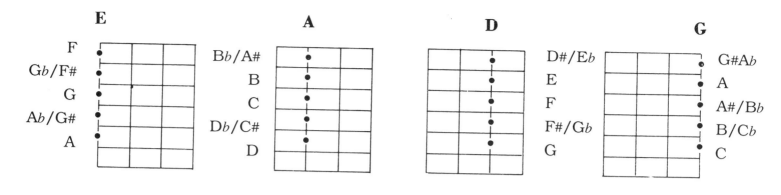

TYPICAL BASS PART, USING SHARPS AND FLATS

At this stage we recommend the student use his own judgment as to fingering.

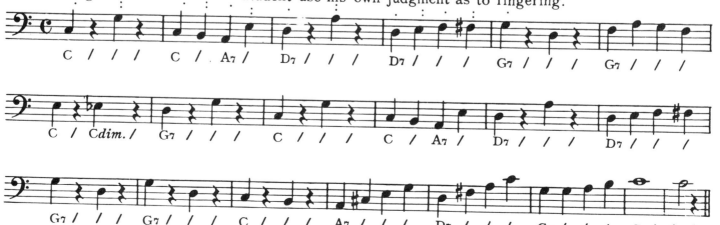

THE EIGHTH NOTE

An eighth note receives one-half beat. (One quarter note equals two eighth notes.)

An eighth note will have a head, stem, and flag. If two or more are in successive order they may be connected by a bar.

Eighth Notes and Eighth Rests

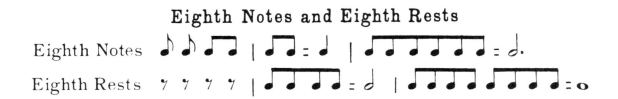

COMPARISON OF RELATED NOTE VALUES and COUNTING EXAMPLE and PRACTISE

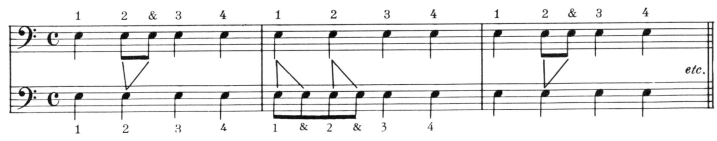

EXAMPLE– USING EIGHTH NOTES

The Dotted Quarter Note (♩·)

The dot increases a note by half of its value.

If you will study this chart carefully you will see where the dotted quarter is the same time value as the three eighth notes compared to it.

Alla-Breve Time

When Common time is to be played in a tempo too fast to conveniently count four beats, it is best to count only two beats to each measure.

Each half measure will receive one beat.

This is referred to as "cut" time.

The time signature for Alla-Breve time will be a vertical line drawn through the letter C as shown: ₵

Twelve Bar Boogie in C

Moderato – to lively

More Boogie in C

The Key of G

ONE ♯ (F♯)

IT IS IDENTIFIED THUS =
ALL F's ARE ♯ (SHARP)

The G Scale

The whole step from 6 (E) to 7 (F♯) causes the F to be sharped . . . . . Thus F♯ in the Signature.

Thirds in G

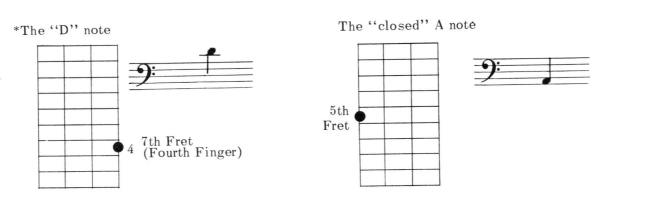

Fingering as in Scale.   No Open Strings.

*The "D" note

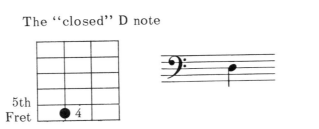

The "closed" A note

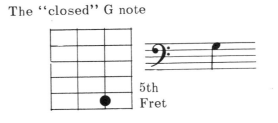

The "closed" D note

The "closed" G note

Eight to the Bar Boogie in G*

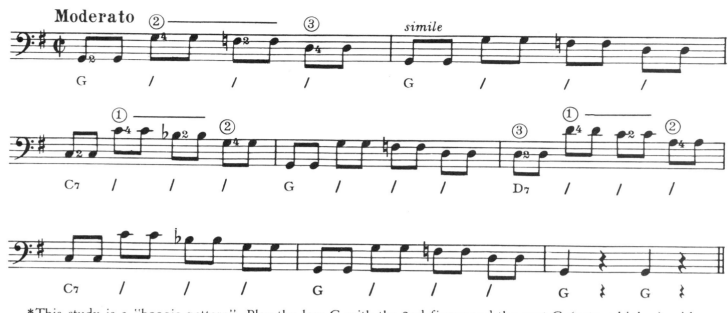

*This study is a "boogie pattern". Play the low G with the 2nd finger and the next G (octave higher) with the 4th finger on the 5th fret of the D or 2nd string. Play F natural with 2nd finger and the "D" with 4th finger on the 3rd (A str.) Use this same fingering pattern beginning with C in 3rd measure through 4th measure and use this same fingering beginning with D on 3rd string. Study this pattern carefully. Most Boogie and Blues patterns employ this fingering and do NOT use any open strings.
(You may substitute the 1st and 3rd fingers in place of the suggested fingering if easier.)

More Eight Bar Boogie (swing) try straight time also

Eight Bar Blues in G

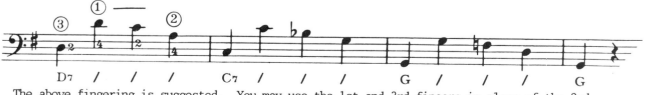

The above fingering is suggested. You may use the 1st and 3rd fingers in place of the 2nd and 4th if easier. Use what is best for you.

Standard Boogie Beat

Follow same fingering patterns as per previous page.

Fingering as above

See ★ at bottom for
this measure.

FINGERING 2   1 2 3 4 3 4   HALF REST

In this Boogie Pattern we introduce the ♮ Natural (or cancellation) sign, which cancels any previous sharp or flat in the signature or in the measure and restores the note to its normal position.

Also introduced in the last measure is the half rest, two counts.

Daily Drilling

Follow same fingering patterns as per previous page.

Do this study first with open strings and then without open strings.

★ The G♯ and A on the sixth and seventh frets help to keep the pattern of this boogie the same fingering as all the other measures. The G♯ and A are the same as the first and second frets on G String.
F♯, G, G♯, A are all played on D String, on fourth, fifth, sixth and seventh frets.

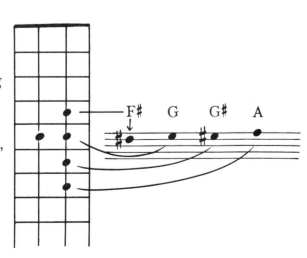

The Scale of F Major
(B♭)
ALL B's ARE FLAT

FINGERING   1   3   0   1   3   0   2   3   0   1   2

The B♭ in this scale is brought about by the ½ step from the third to the fourth note of the scale. From A to B♭ is a half step.

Arpeggio Study
USING THE THREE PRINCIPAL CHORDS IN THIS KEY

F / /   F / /   B♭ / /   B♭ / /   C / /   C / /   F / /   F—

Scale Pattern

Study in Thirds
KEY OF "F"

More Study of Thirds in F Major

Use same fingering as in the F Major scale.

→ play with metronome
& without
→ steady/even tempo

Italian Boat Song

Study in Fifths

The Triplet

Triplets are a group of three notes played in the same time as two of its own denomination. Thus [notation] would be played in the same time as [notation]

Count 1 - tri - plet   2 - tri - plet   3 - tri - plet   4

Thinking of a three syllable word can help immeasureably in getting the right division.

We recommend **1** Triplet, **2** Triplet.

RHYTHM AND BLUES PATTERN, USING DIMINISHED CHORD

G / G♯° / Am / D₇ /

Two "Circle of Sixths" Patterns

G / Em / C / D₇ /

C / Am / F / G₇ /

Example
USING F♯ AND MORE EIGHTH NOTES

Count 1 2 3 4 &

1 2 3 4 & 1 2 3 4

[final staff line]

From here on the F♯ will be indicated in the Key Signature only when playing in the Key of G.

*See Page 24 for this note. (D)

30

The Sixteenth Note

Thus you can see that it takes four sixteenth notes to make a quarter.

Count   1 – six – teenth–notes 2 – six – teenth–notes 3 – six – teenth–notes 4 – six – teenth–notes

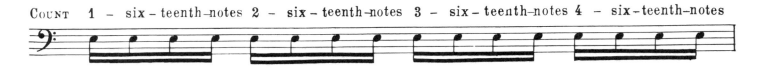

More in C

1st POS.

Slow

C   /   Am   /   Dm   /   G7   /
Count   1   2   &   ah   3   4   &

C   /   Am   /   Dm   /   G7   /

Still More in C

1st POS.

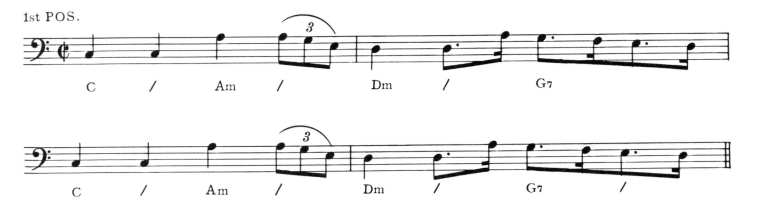

C   /   Am   /   Dm   /   G7

C   /   Am   /   Dm   /   G7   /

Rock and Roll– Rhythm and Blues– Boogie Patterns

Do not use open strings in this and all following Rock and Roll, Rhythm and Blues, and Boogie patterns. By so doing the patterns become movable.

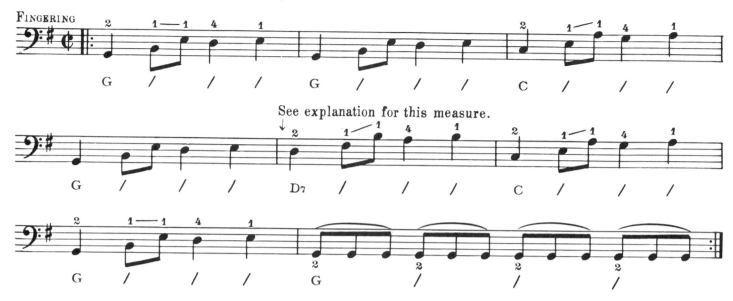

See explanation for this measure.

In the fifth measure of this pattern we use the same fingering as in the first measure. This is a pattern and by using the same fingering and by not using open strings this pattern becomes movable and can be played in many keys by simply beginning the pattern on higher frets; for example by beginning on the 4th fret you are in A♭: 6th fret B♭: 8th fret C; etc.

The expert Bassist will recognize the value of not using the open strings. The Bass beginner who has not played the guitar previously should, with a little effort, be able to understand this explanation.

Four Bar Blues Pattern in C

Play dotted ⅛ and 1/16 with a bounce counting a long one and a short &.

BASS PARTS

The average bass part will use the root (x) and the 5th (0) of the chord.

The diagrams shown here can be used as a bass part to all of the following chords:

C Major	C Maj. 7	C mi 9	C 11	C $\frac{9}{6}$
C Minor	C Min. 7	C Maj 9	C 11 +	
C Seventh	C 6	C − 9	C 13	
C Ninth	C Mi 6	C 9 +	C 13−9	

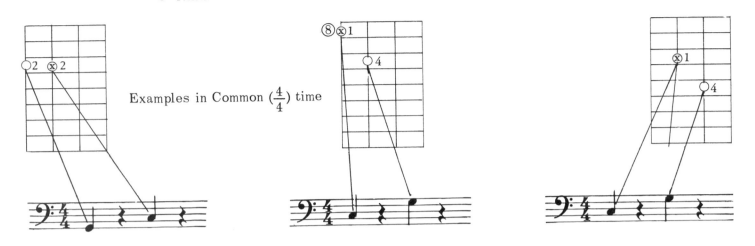

These diagrams can be used as bass parts to the following chords:

⊗ - Root
○ - 5th

C Aug   C7th#5   C9th#5

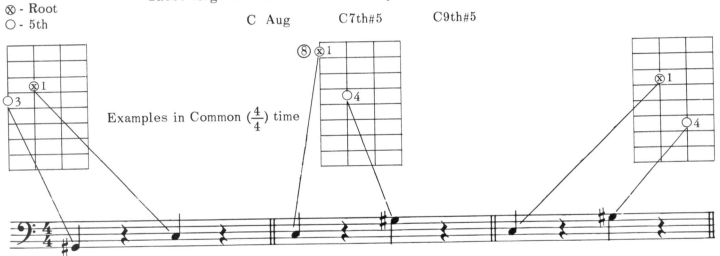

These diagrams can be used as bass part to the following chords:

⊗ - Root
○ - 5th

C dim.   C7th ♭5   C9th ♭5   C13th-9 ♭5

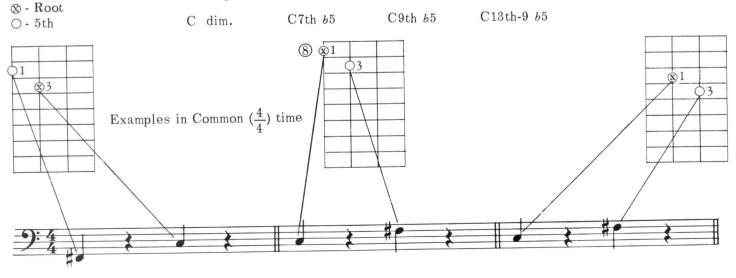

The following diagrams may be used
as bass parts to the above chords.

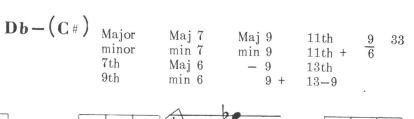

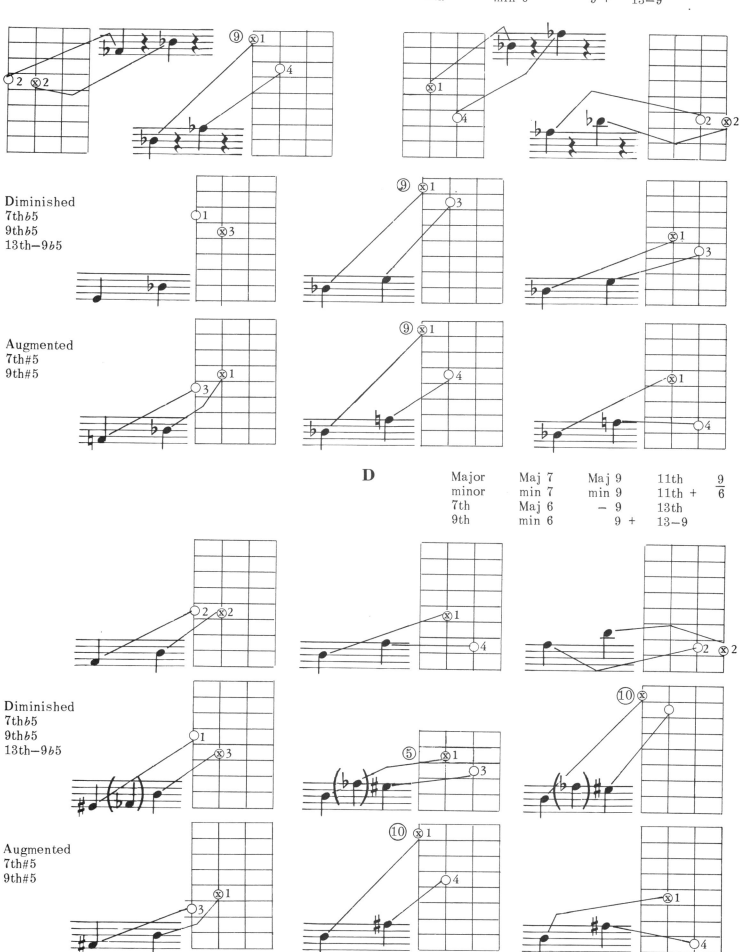

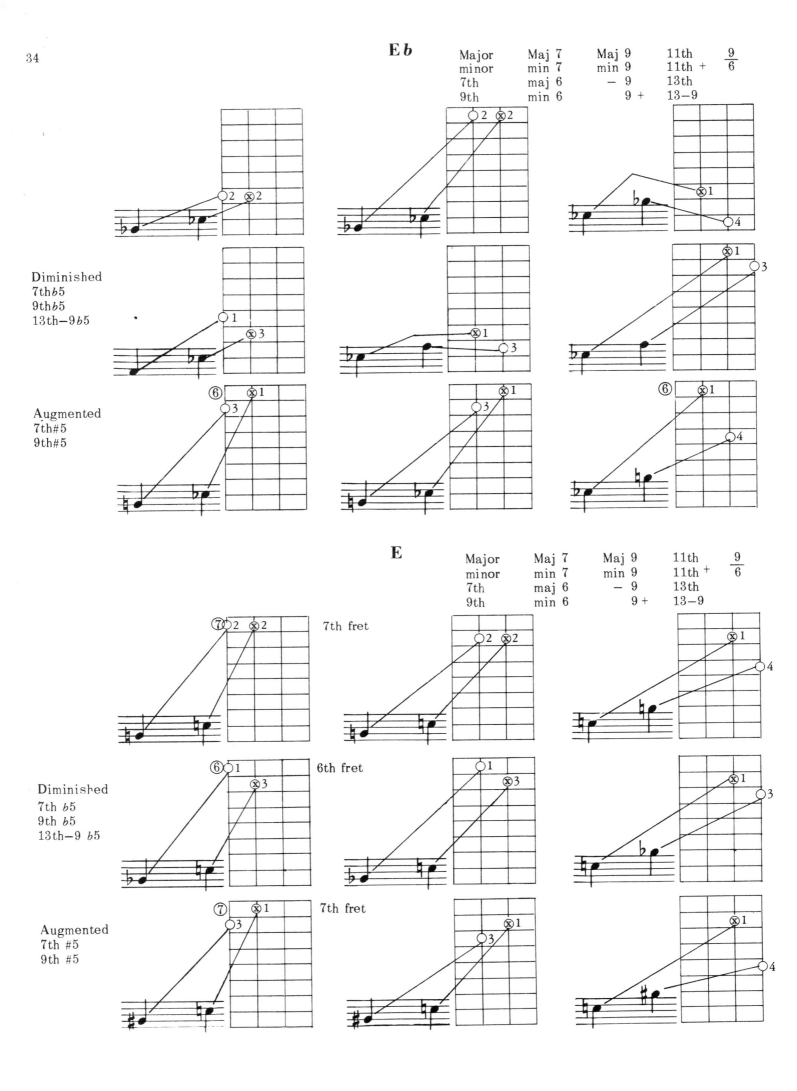

E♭

Major	Maj 7	Maj 9	11th	$\frac{9}{6}$
minor	min 7	min 9	11th +	
7th	maj 6	− 9	13th	
9th	min 6	9 +	13−9	

Diminished
7th♭5
9th♭5
13th−9♭5

Augmented
7th#5
9th#5

E

Major	Maj 7	Maj 9	11th	$\frac{9}{6}$
minor	min 7	min 9	11th +	
7th	maj 6	− 9	13th	
9th	min 6	9 +	13−9	

7th fret

Diminished
7th ♭5
9th ♭5
13th−9 ♭5

6th fret

Augmented
7th #5
9th #5

7th fret

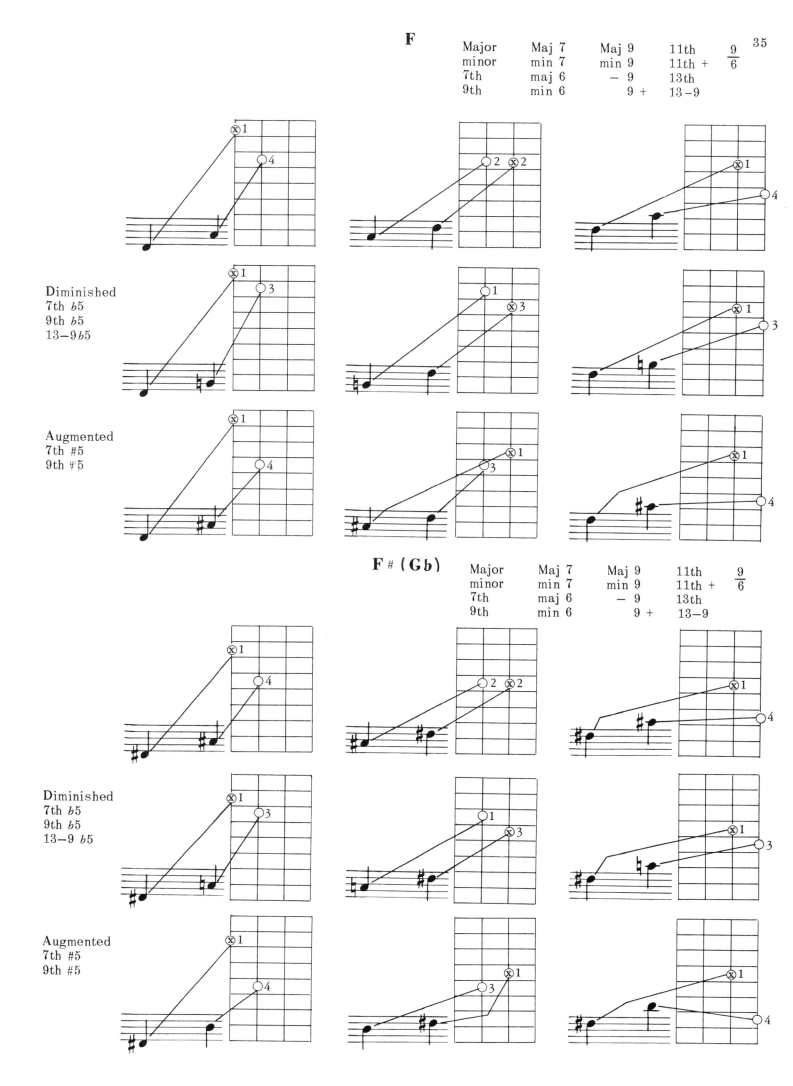

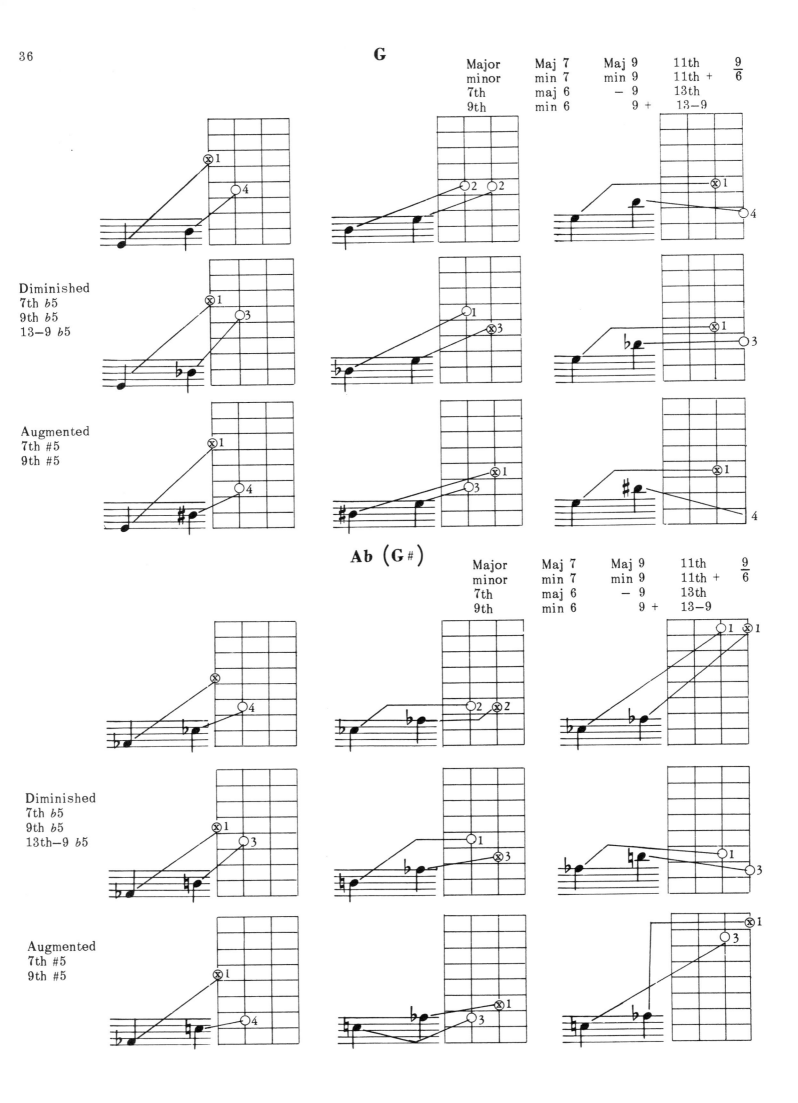

G

Major	Maj 7	Maj 9	11th	$\frac{9}{6}$
minor	min 7	min 9	11th +	
7th	maj 6	– 9	13th	
9th	min 6	9 +	13–9	

Diminished
7th b5
9th b5
13–9 b5

Augmented
7th #5
9th #5

Ab (G#)

Major	Maj 7	Maj 9	11th	$\frac{9}{6}$
minor	min 7	min 9	11th +	
7th	maj 6	– 9	13th	
9th	min 6	9 +	13–9	

Diminished
7th b5
9th b5
13th–9 b5

Augmented
7th #5
9th #5

A

Major	Maj 7	Maj 9	11th	9/6
minor	mi 7	mi 9	11th +	
7th	Maj 6	9th	13th	
9th	mi 6	9+	13−9	

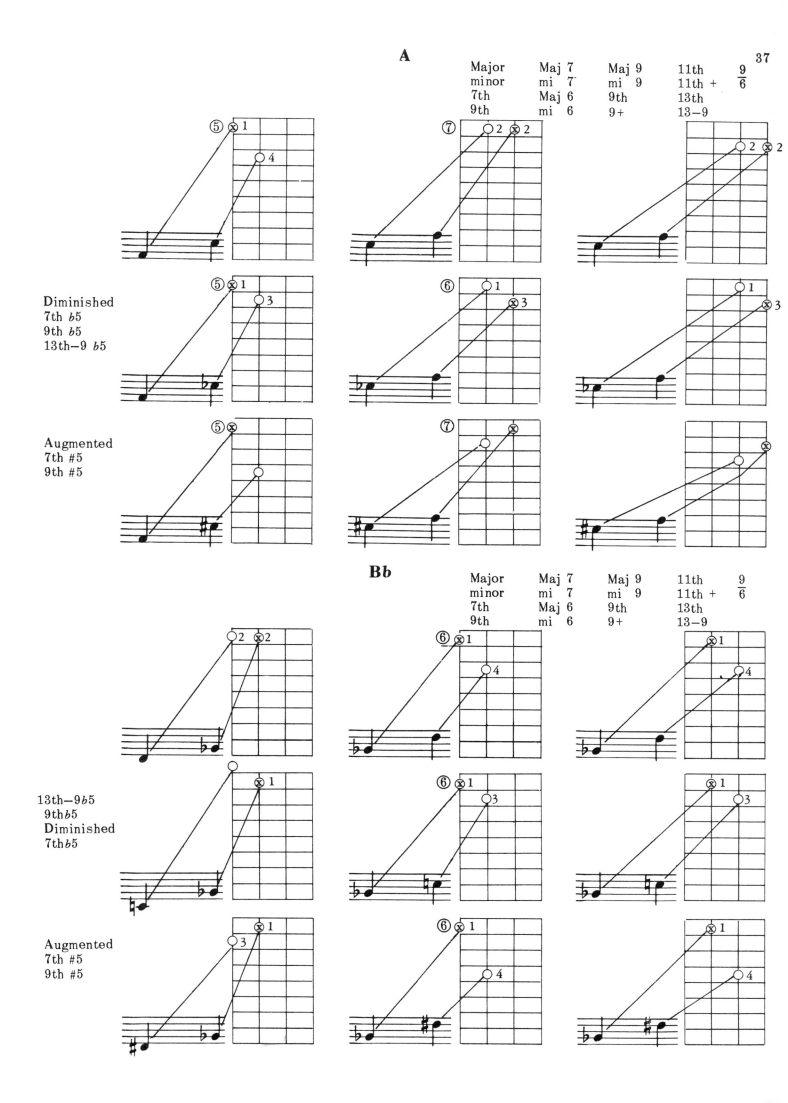

Diminished
7th ♭5
9th ♭5
13th−9 ♭5

Augmented
7th #5
9th #5

Bb

Major	Maj 7	Maj 9	11th	9/6
minor	mi 7	mi 9	11th +	
7th	Maj 6	9th	13th	
9th	mi 6	9+	13−9	

13th−9♭5
9th♭5
Diminished
7th♭5

Augmented
7th #5
9th #5

B (C♭)

Major	Maj 7	mi 9th	11th	$\dfrac{9}{6}$
minor	mi 7	maj 9th	11th +	
Seventh	Sixth	ninth	13th	
Ninth	Mi 6th	9 +	13−9	

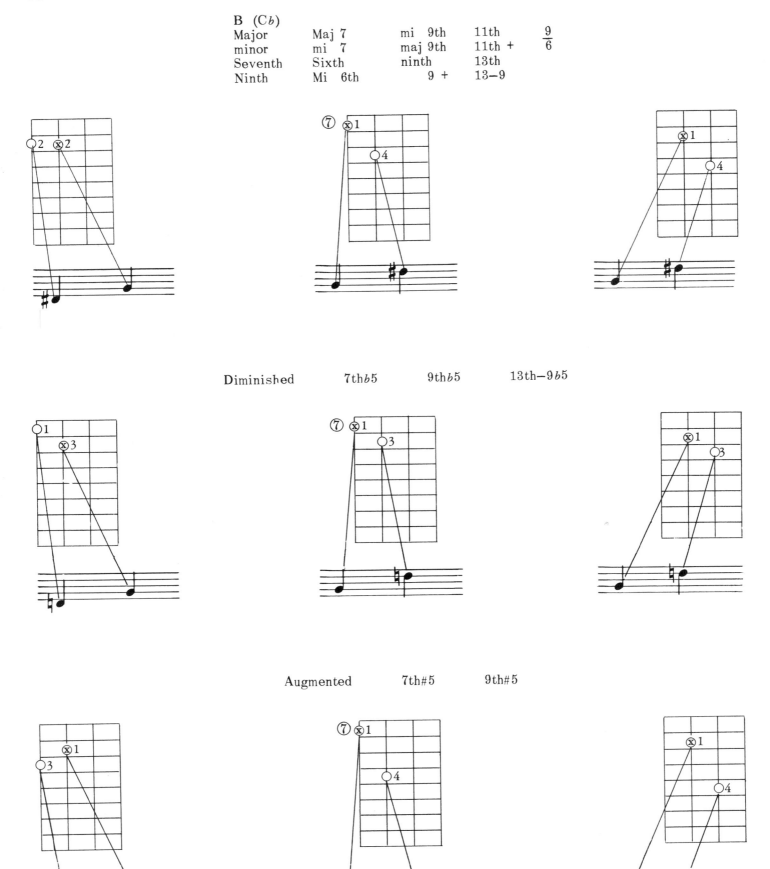

Diminished   7th♭5   9th♭5   13th−9♭5

Augmented   7th#5   9th#5

Application of these forms is the same as on the "C" pages

The Major Chord Arpeggios

These forms are movable and should be practiced from the first to the twelfth fret.
The fret location is determined by the first finger

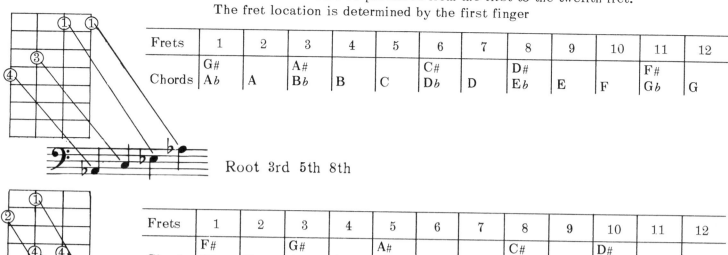

Frets	1	2	3	4	5	6	7	8	9	10	11	12
Chords	G# Ab	A	A# Bb	B	C	C# Db	D	D# Eb	E	F	F# Gb	G

Root 3rd 5th 8th

Frets	1	2	3	4	5	6	7	8	9	10	11	12
Chords	F# Gb	G	G# Ab	A	A# Bb	B	C	C# Db	D	D# Eb	E	F

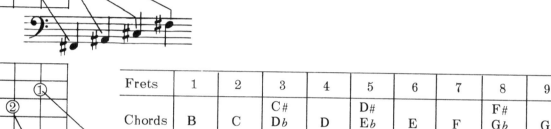

Frets	1	2	3	4	5	6	7	8	9	10	11	12
Chords	B	C	C# Db	D	D# Eb	E	F	F# Gb	G	G# Ab	A	A# Bb

All arpeggios should be
practiced in this order.

The Major Seventh Arpeggio

The Minor 9th Arpeggio (minus root)

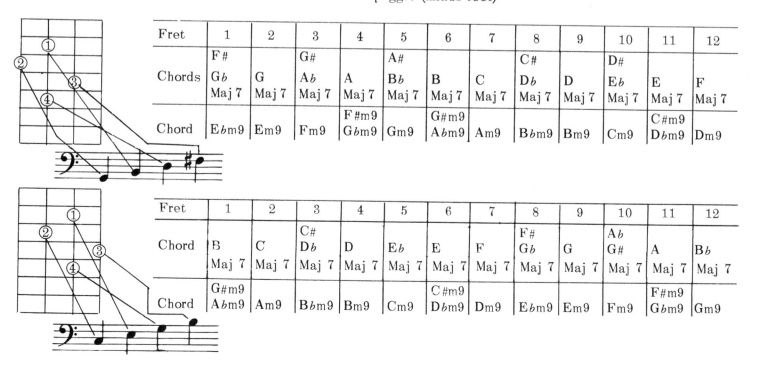

Fret	1	2	3	4	5	6	7	8	9	10	11	12
Chords	F# Gb Maj 7	G Maj 7	G# Ab Maj 7	A Maj 7	A# Bb Maj 7	B Maj 7	C Maj 7	C# Db Maj 7	D Maj 7	D# Eb Maj 7	E Maj 7	F Maj 7
Chord	Ebm9	Em9	Fm9	F#m9 Gbm9	Gm9	G#m9 Abm9	Am9	Bbm9	Bm9	Cm9	C#m9 Dbm9	Dm9

Fret	1	2	3	4	5	6	7	8	9	10	11	12
Chord	B Maj 7	C Maj 7	C# Db Maj 7	D Maj 7	Eb Maj 7	E Maj 7	F Maj 7	F# Gb Maj 7	G Maj 7	Ab G# Maj 7	A Maj 7	Bb Maj 7
Chord	G#m9 Abm9	Am9	Bbm9	Bm9	Cm9	C#m9 Dbm9	Dm9	Ebm9	Em9	Fm9	F#m9 Gbm9	Gm9

The Dominant Seventh Chord Arpeggio

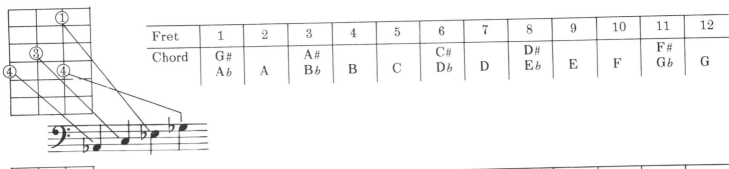

Fret	1	2	3	4	5	6	7	8	9	10	11	12
Chord	G# Ab	A	A# Bb	B	C	C# Db	D	D# Eb	E	F	F# Gb	G

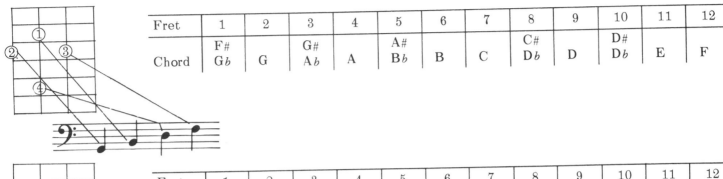

Fret	1	2	3	4	5	6	7	8	9	10	11	12
Chord	F# Gb	G	G# Ab	A	A# Bb	B	C	C# Db	D	D# Db	E	F

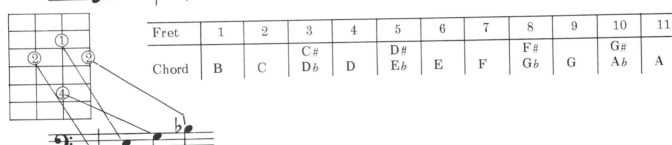

Fret	1	2	3	4	5	6	7	8	9	10	11	12
Chord	B	C	C# Db	D	D# Eb	E	F	F# Gb	G	G# Ab	A	A# Bb

The Major Sixth Arpeggio

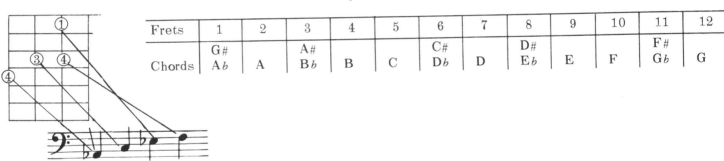

Frets	1	2	3	4	5	6	7	8	9	10	11	12
Chords	G# Ab	A	A# Bb	B	C	C# Db	D	D# Eb	E	F	F# Gb	G

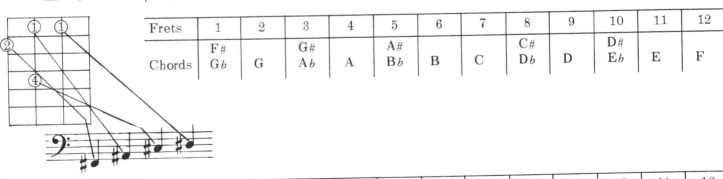

Frets	1	2	3	4	5	6	7	8	9	10	11	12
Chords	F# Gb	G	G# Ab	A	A# Bb	B	C	C# Db	D	D# Eb	E	F

Frets	1	2	3	4	5	6	7	8	9	10	11	12
Chords	B	C	C# Db	D	D# Eb	E	F	F# Gb	G	G# Ab	A	A# Bb

The Minor Chord Arpeggio

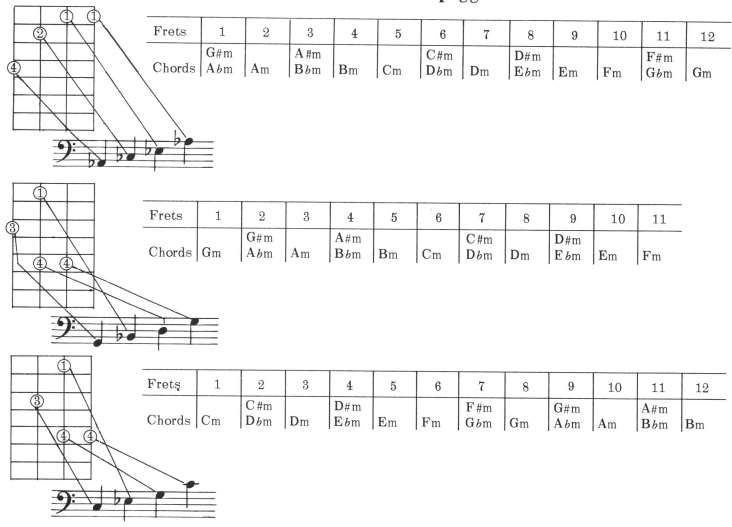

Frets	1	2	3	4	5	6	7	8	9	10	11	12
Chords	G#m Abm	Am	A#m Bbm	Bm	Cm	C#m Dbm	Dm	D#m Ebm	Em	Fm	F#m Gbm	Gm

Frets	1	2	3	4	5	6	7	8	9	10	11
Chords	Gm	G#m Abm	Am	A#m Bbm	Bm	Cm	C#m Dbm	Dm	D#m Ebm	Em	Fm

Frets	1	2	3	4	5	6	7	8	9	10	11	12
Chords	Cm	C#m Dbm	Dm	D#m Ebm	Em	Fm	F#m Gbm	Gm	G#m Abm	Am	A#m Bbm	Bm

The Minor Seventh Arpeggio

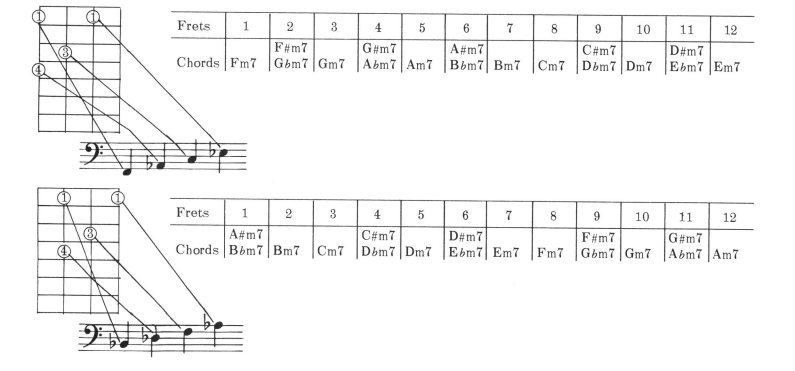

Frets	1	2	3	4	5	6	7	8	9	10	11	12
Chords	Fm7	F#m7 Gbm7	Gm7	G#m7 Abm7	Am7	A#m7 Bbm7	Bm7	Cm7	C#m7 Dbm7	Dm7	D#m7 Ebm7	Em7

Frets	1	2	3	4	5	6	7	8	9	10	11	12
Chords	A#m7 Bbm7	Bm7	Cm7	C#m7 Dbm7	Dm7	D#m7 Ebm7	Em7	Fm7	F#m7 Gbm7	Gm7	G#m7 Abm7	Am7

The Minor Sixth Chord Arpeggio

The Ninth Chord Arpeggio (minus root)

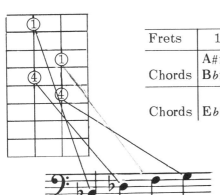

Frets	1	2	3	4	5	6	7	8	9	10	11	12
Chords	Fm6	F#m6 Gbm6	Gm6	G#m6 Abm6	Am6	A#m6 Bbm6	Bm6	Cm6	C#m6 Dbm6	Dm6	D#m6 Ebm6	Em6
Chords	A#9 Bb9	B9	C9	C#9 Db9	D9	D#9 Eb9	E9	F9	F#9 Gb9	G9	G#9 Ab9	A9

Frets	1	2	3	4	5	6	7	8	9	10	11	12
Chords	A#m6 Bbm6	Bm6	Cm6	C#m6 Dbm6	Dm6	D#m6 Ebm6	Em6	Fm6	F#m6 Gbm6	Gm6	G#m6 Abm6	Am6
Chords	Eb9	E9	F9	F#9 Gb9	G9	G#9 Ab9	A9	A#9 Bb9	B9	C9	D#9 Db9	D9

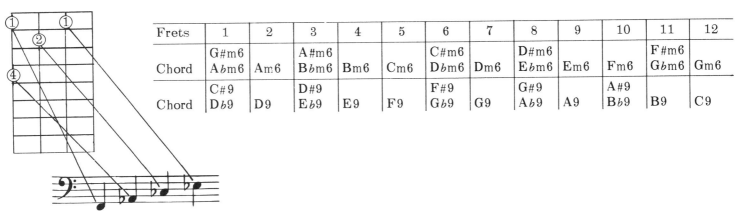

Minor Sixth Arpeggio (Continued)

Dominant Ninth Arpeggio (minus root)

Frets	1	2	3	4	5	6	7	8	9	10	11	12
Chord	G#m6 Abm6	Am6	A#m6 Bbm6	Bm6	Cm6	C#m6 Dbm6	Dm6	D#m6 Ebm6	Em6	Fm6	F#m6 Gbm6	Gm6
Chord	C#9 Db9	D9	D#9 Eb9	E9	F9	F#9 Gb9	G9	G#9 Ab9	A9	A#9 Bb9	B9	C9

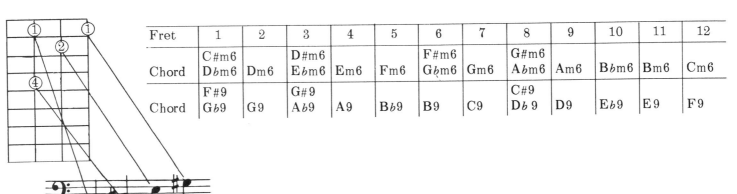

Fret	1	2	3	4	5	6	7	8	9	10	11	12
Chord	C#m6 Dbm6	Dm6	D#m6 Ebm6	Em6	Fm6	F#m6 Gbm6	Gm6	G#m6 Abm6	Am6	Bbm6	Bm6	Cm6
Chord	F#9 Gb9	G9	G#9 Ab9	A9	Bb9	B9	C9	C#9 Db9	D9	Eb9	E9	F9

The Diminished Chord Arpeggio

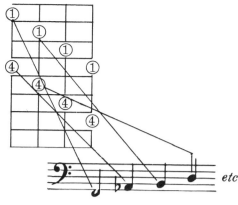

Frets	1	2	3	4	5	6	7	8	9	10
Chords	F	F#	G	F	F#	G	F	F#	G	F
	G#	A	Bb	G#	A	Bb	G#	A	Bb	G#
	Ab	C	C#	Ab	C	C#	Ab	C	C#	Ab
	B	Eb	E	B	Eb	E	B	Eb	E	B
	Cb	Gb	A#	Cb	Gb	A#	Cb	Gb	A#	Cb
	D	B#	Db	D	B#	Db	D	B#	Db	D
	E#	D#		E#	D#		E#	D#		E#

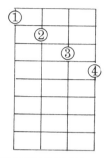

The Augmented Chord Arpeggio

Frets	1	2	3	4	5	6	7	8	9	10	11	12
Chords	Ab	A	Bb	B	Ab	A	Bb	B	Ab	A	Bb	B
	C	C#	D	D#	C	C#	D	D#	C	C#	D	D#
	E	E#	F#	G	E	E#	F#	G	E	E#	F#	G
	G#	F	Gb	Eb	G#	F	Gb	Eb	G#	F	Gb	Eb
	B#	Db			B#	Db			B#	Db		

The Seventh b5

The 9 + 5 (9 # 5)

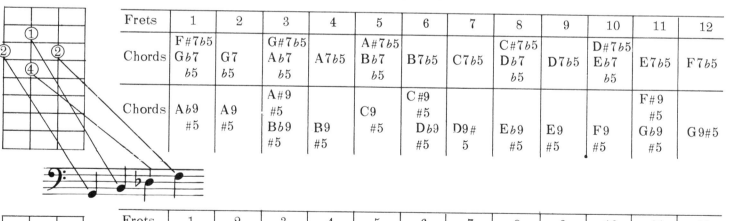

Frets	1	2	3	4	5	6	7	8	9	10	11	12
Chords	F#7b5		G#7b5		A#7b5			C#7b5		D#7b5		
	Gb7 b5	G7 b5	Ab7 b5	A7b5	Bb7 b5	B7b5	C7b5	Db7 b5	D7b5	Eb7 b5	E7b5	F7b5
Chords	Ab9 #5	A9 #5	A#9 #5 / Bb9 #5	B9 #5	C9 #5	C#9 #5 / Db9 #5	D9# 5	Eb9 #5	E9 #5	F9 #5	F#9 #5 / Gb9 #5	G9#5

Frets	1	2	3	4	5	6	7	8	9	10	11	12
Chords			C#7 b5		D#7 b5			F#7 b5		G#7 b5		A#7b5
	B7b5	C7 b5	Db7 b5	D7 b5	Eb7 b5	E7 b5	F7 b5	Gb7 b5	G7 b5	Ab7 b5	A7 b5	Bb7b5
	Db9 #5	D9#5	Eb9 #5	E9 #5	F9 #5	F#9 #5 / Gb9 #5	G9 #5 / G#9 #5	Ab9 #5	A9 #5	Bb9 #5	B9 #5	C9#5

The Seventh +5 Chord
(#5)

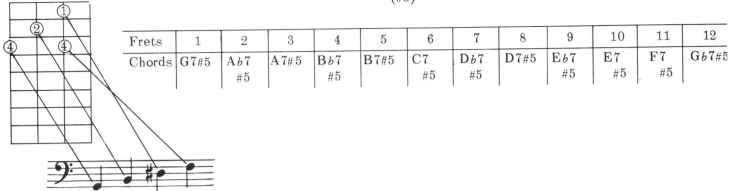

Frets	1	2	3	4	5	6	7	8	9	10	11	12
Chords	G7#5	Ab7 #5	A7#5	Bb7 #5	B7#5	C7 #5	Db7 #5	D7#5	Eb7 #5	E7 #5	F7 #5	Gb7#5

Frets	1	2	3	4	5	6	7	8	9	10	11	12
Chords	C7#5	C#7 #5 / Db7 #5	D7 5	D#7 #5 / Eb7 #5	E7#5	F7#5	F#7 #5 / Gb7 #5	G7#5	G#7 #5 / Ab7 #5	A7#5	A#7 #5 / Bb7 #5	B7 #5

The 9–5 Chord Arpeggio
(b5)

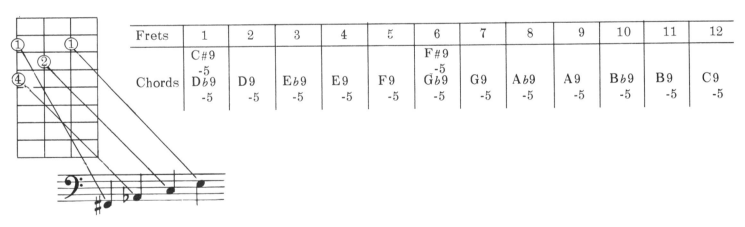

Frets	1	2	3	4	5	6	7	8	9	10	11	12
Chords	C#9 -5 / Db9 -5	D9 -5	Eb9 -5	E9 -5	F9 -5	F#9 -5 / Gb9 -5	G9 -5	Ab9 -5	A9 -5	Bb9 -5	B9 -5	C9 -5

Frets	1	2	3	4	5	6	7	8	9	10	11	12
Chords	F#9 -5 / Gb9 -5	G9 -5	Ab9 -5	A9 -5	Bb9 -5	B9 -5	C9 -5	C#9 -5 / Db9 -5	D9 -5	Eb9 -5	E9 -5	F9 -5

The Minus Ninth Chord Arpeggio
(7♭9 or 7 -9)

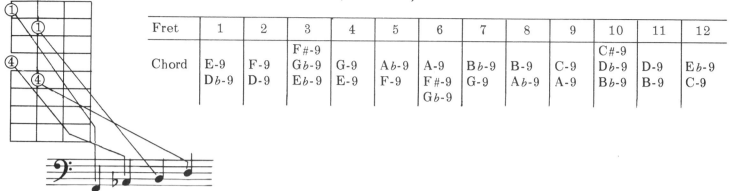

Fret	1	2	3	4	5	6	7	8	9	10	11	12
Chord	E-9 D♭-9	F-9 D-9	F#-9 G♭-9 E♭-9	G-9 E-9	A♭-9 F-9	A-9 F#-9 G♭-9	B♭-9 G-9	B-9 A♭-9	C-9 A-9	C#-9 D♭-9 B♭-9	D-9 B-9	E♭-9 C-9

Fret	1	2	3	4	5	6	7	8	9	10	11	12
Chord	F-9 D-9	F#-9 G♭-9 E♭-9	G-9 E-9	A♭-9 F-9	A-9 F#-9 G♭-9	B♭-9 G-9	B-9 A♭-9	C-9 A-9	C#-9 D♭-9 B♭-9	D-9 B-9	E♭-9 C-9	E-9 D♭-9 C#-9

The Major Ninth Chord Arpeggio

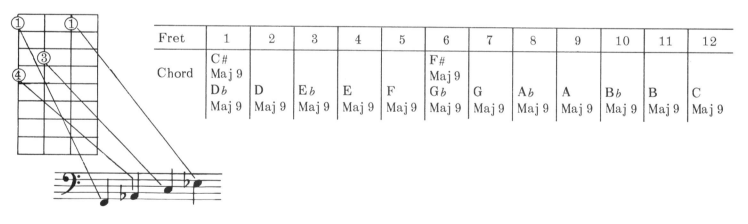

Fret	1	2	3	4	5	6	7	8	9	10	11	12
Chord	C# Maj 9 D♭ Maj 9	D Maj 9	E♭ Maj 9	E Maj 9	F Maj 9	F# Maj 9 G♭ Maj 9	G Maj 9	A♭ Maj 9	A Maj 9	B♭ Maj 9	B Maj 9	C Maj 9

Fret	1	2	3	4	5	6	7	8	9	10	11	12
Chord	F# Maj 9 G♭ Maj 9	G Maj 9	A♭ Maj 9	A Maj 9	B♭ Maj 9	B Maj 9	C Maj 9	C# Maj 9 D♭ Maj 9	D Maj 9	E♭ Maj 9	E Maj 9	F Maj 9

The Augmented Ninth Chord Arpeggio

(9 +)

(Sometimes shown 7th #9)

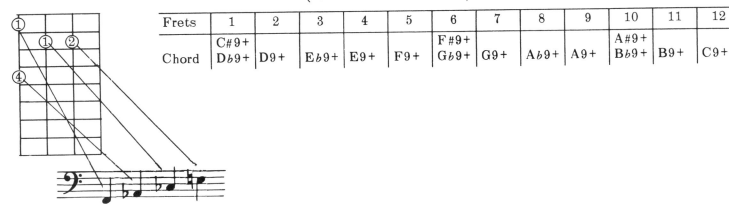

Frets	1	2	3	4	5	6	7	8	9	10	11	12
Chord	C#9+ D♭9+	D9+	E♭9+	E9+	F9+	F#9+ G♭9+	G9+	A♭9+	A9+	A#9+ B♭9+	B9+	C9+

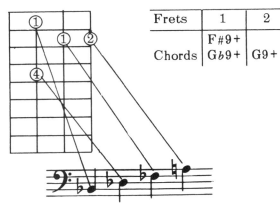

Frets	1	2	3	4	5	6	7	8	9	10	11	12
Chords	F#9+ G♭9+	G9+	A♭9+	A9+	B♭9+	B9+	C9+	C#9+ D♭9+	D9+	E♭9+	E9+	F9+

The Eleventh Chord

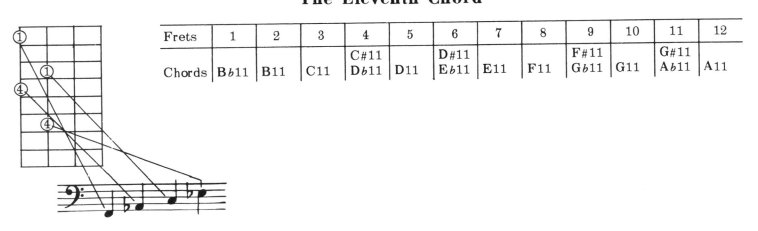

Frets	1	2	3	4	5	6	7	8	9	10	11	12
Chords	B♭11	B11	C11	C#11 D♭11	D11	D#11 E♭11	E11	F11	F#11 G♭11	G11	G#11 A♭11	A11

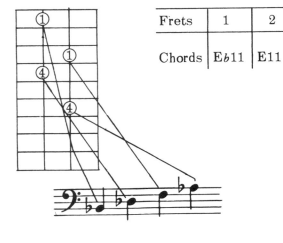

Frets	1	2	3	4	5	6	7	8	9	10	11	12
Chords	E♭11	E11	F11	F#11 G♭11	G11	G#11 A♭11	A11	B♭11	B11	C11	C#11 D♭11	D11

The $\frac{9}{6}$ Chord Arpeggio

This chord is used chiefly at endings.

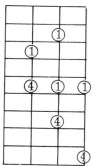

Fret	1	2	3	4	5	6	7
Chord	F#$\frac{6}{9}$ G♭$\frac{9}{6}$	G$\frac{9}{6}$	A♭$\frac{9}{6}$	A$\frac{9}{6}$	B♭$\frac{9}{6}$	B$\frac{9}{6}$	C$\frac{9}{6}$

Fret	1	2	3	4	5	6	7
Chord	B$\frac{9}{6}$	C$\frac{9}{6}$	D♭$\frac{9}{6}$ C#$\frac{9}{6}$	D$\frac{9}{6}$	E♭$\frac{9}{6}$	E$\frac{9}{6}$	F$\frac{9}{6}$

THE THIRTEENTH CHORD

Substitute the 7th or 9th of the same name. Ex: F13 — Use F7th or F9th.

THE SUSPENSION

Symbol (sus). Use the Eleventh of the same name Ex: D7th Sus. use D11th.

THE AUGMENTED ELEVENTH

Symbol 11 +. Use the Ninth ♭5 Arpeggio of the same name. Ex: Caug 11 use C9 ♭5 Arp.

THE THIRTEENTH MINUS (-) 9 CHORD

Symbol 13-9. Use the 7-9 as a substitute.

An Orchestration Style

Employing the GUITAR PART with BASS NOTATION below as actually played.

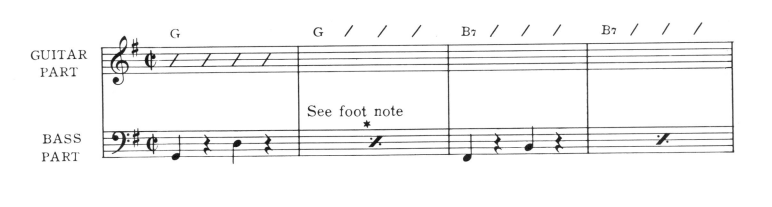

See foot note
*

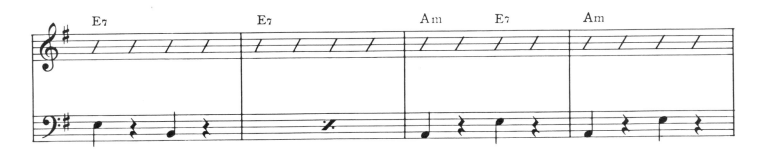

* This Sign- ⅞ means to repeat the previous measure.